The 20-Minute Bible Study Workbook

The 20-Minute Bible Study Workbook

Volume 3 – 13 Weeks

Mark, 1 & 2 Corinthians, 2 Samuel

J. A. Marucci
R. K. Brownrigg

© 2023 by John A. Marucci

Published by Happy Tent Media Group, LLC
6749 S Westnedge Ave, Suite K #304
Portage, Michigan 49002-3556

All rights reserved. No part of this publication may be reproduced, stored in a retrieval system, or transmitted in any form or by any means without the prior written permission of the publisher. The only exception is brief quotations for printed reviews.

Unless otherwise indicated, Scripture quotations are from The Holy Bible, English Standard Version®, copyright © 2001 by Crossway Bibles, a publishing ministry of Good News Publishers. Used by permission. All rights reserved.

Cover Photo: Yosemite Valley, California
Photo by Max Pruvost on Unsplash

INTRODUCTION

This Bible study workbook has been carefully designed and refined over many years to help you effectively learn what the Bible says. The workbook is set up for Monday through Saturday use, and a day's reading and answering questions will usually take about 20 minutes. It is primarily designed for personal study but can be adapted for small group use.

Try to set aside the same time each day. If you are a morning person, try to do this first thing. Not everyone is a morning person, and many people prefer later in the day, evening, or during a lunch break. Whenever the best time of day is for you, try to set aside the same time daily.

To get the most out of this workbook, you will want to read the daily assigned reading and write down your answers to the questions presented. You can write in the workbook, as there is space under each question to write down answers.

It is normal to miss a time or two for various reasons. Don't let missing discourage you from picking it back up. If you miss a day or even a week, start again with the next day's reading or the beginning of the following week.

Finally, your positive rating and a written review of this workbook will make it more readily available for others to find and use. If you find this workbook helpful, please consider taking a moment and posting a review on Amazon.com.

Thank you, and God bless you as you study the Bible!

J. A. Marucci
R. K. Brownrigg

Name:_____ Date Started: _____

Weekly Checklist/Contents:

- [ ] Week 1 (Page 9) — Mark 1 – Mark 3
- [ ] Week 2 (Page 15) — Mark 4 – Mark 7
- [ ] Week 3 (Page 21) — Mark 8 – Mark 10
- [ ] Week 4 (Page 27) — Mark 11 – Mark 16
- [ ] Week 5 (Page 33) — 1 Corinthians 1 – 1 Corinthians 6
- [ ] Week 6 (Page 39) — 1 Corinthians 7 – 1 Corinthians 11
- [ ] Week 7 (Page 45) — 1 Corinthians 12 – 1 Corinthians 16
- [ ] Week 8 (Page 51) — 2 Corinthians 1 – 2 Corinthians 6
- [ ] Week 9 (Page 57) — 2 Corinthians 7 – 2 Corinthians 13
- [ ] Week 10 (Page 63) — 2 Samuel 1 – 2 Samuel 6
- [ ] Week 11 (Page 69) — 2 Samuel 7 – 2 Samuel 12
- [ ] Week 12 (Page 75) — 2 Samuel 13 – 2 Samuel 18
- [ ] Week 13 (Page 81) — 2 Samuel 19 – 2 Samuel 24

Weekly Memory Verses (Page 87)

Journal Pages (Page 88)

"...be attentive to my words; incline your ear to my sayings. Let them not escape from your sight; keep them within your heart. For they are life to those who find them, and healing to all their flesh." — Proverbs 4:20-22 (ESV)

Week 1 — This week's Bible reading begins a walk through the Gospel of Mark. We'll look at John the Baptist, Jesus' teaching and healing, Jesus' prayer life, and Jesus being opposed, criticized, and rejected by the teachers of the law and his family.

Monday

Read Mark 1:1–20
What does this passage tell us about the person and ministry of John the Baptist? (Mark 1:2–8)

What did Jesus first preach? (Mark 1:14–15)

galilee - proclaiming the gospel of God → OT prophecies
time is fulfilled
repent & believe in the gospel

What did Jesus promise the fishermen whom He called? How did the fishermen respond? (Mark 1:16–18)

fishers of men
but it says "I will make you"

Tuesday

Read Mark 1:21–34

How did Jesus teach the people? (Mark 1:21–22)

As one, c authority
+ not as the scribes
taught not repeating the traditions or words of others

How did Jesus set the man free in the synagogue? What was the crowd's response? (Mark 1:23–28)

Jesus rebuked the unclean spirits
told devil to hush
the unclean spirit - crying out c a loud voice came out of him

crowd was amazed

What happened at Simon and Andrew's house? What happened that evening? (Mark 1:29–34)

Simon's mother in law was ill c fever / when Jesus took her by the hand - fever left. And she got up & began to serve -

not allow demons to speak because they knew him as holy one of God

Wednesday

Read Mark 1:35–45

What can we learn from verse 35 about Jesus' prayer life? How was His ministry characterized at this point? (Mark 1:35–39)

Alone to pray - desolate place (early in morning)

How did Jesus heal the leper? (Mark 1:41–42)

*Stretched out his hand
touched him -
I will, be clean as He persuaded
if you will you can make me clean -*

What did Jesus tell the leper to do in response to his healing? What did the leper do and how did it affect Jesus' ability to move about? (Mark 1:43–45)

*Show yourself to priest
sent him away at once
say nothing to anyone

Jesus can't stay hidden
my joy at cleansing from sin
should be evident to all. -*

— His steadfast love endures forever —

Thursday

Read Mark 2:1–12

Who brought the paralyzed man to Jesus? How did they get him to Jesus? What does the passage say about how Jesus responded to their faith? (Mark 2:1–5)

when Jesus saw their faith - ones who carried the man - 4 people.

he said - [SON] - your sins are forgiven

How did the scribes respond to Jesus' proclamation of the man's forgiveness? (Mark 2:6–7)

? in ♡ but Jesus knew - perceiving in his spirit

Show Jesus has <u>authority</u> to forgive sins

said: Rise
pick up your bed
go home

How did Jesus respond to the criticism from the scribes? What happened to the paralyzed man? (Mark 2:8–12)

Friday

Read Mark 2:13–27

Where did Jesus and His disciples go after Levi was called? Who was with them? (Mark 2:15)

his house : reclined at the table

tax collectors & sinners

How did the scribes of the Pharisees respond to Jesus' conduct? How did Jesus respond to their criticism? (Mark 2:16–17)

well need no physician / but sick
I came to sinners

① are far from me –
fear is a command taught by men ⟩ NO
I will do wonderful things to these people
meek obtain fresh joy in the Lord

What were the Pharisees critical about and how did Jesus reply to them? (Mark 2:23–28)

Saturday

Read Mark 3

What was the backdrop for the healing of the man with the withered hand? What is told about Jesus' feelings toward those who were looking for a reason to accuse Him? (Mark 3:1–6)

The synagogue people watched Jesus silently to his ?? about lawful Sabbath
saw hardness of heart
Jesus was angry but grieved
pharisees were the ones

"Stretch out your hand."

Why did Jesus appoint the Twelve? Who were they? (Mark 3:13–19)

unclean spirits knew Him
you are the Son of God
may be with him / sent them to preach
& have authority to cast out demons

Why did Jesus' mother and brothers come to see Him? What did His family think of Jesus at the time? What did the scribes think of Him and His ministry at the time? (Mark 3:20–22)

could not eat - crowd
family heard, went to
seize him, he is
"out of his mind"
possessed by demon
who does God's will is brother, sister + mother

You keep her in perfect peace whose mind is stayed on you, because she trusts in you. Trust forever

Week 2 — This week's Bible reading continues a walk through the Gospel of Mark. We will look at some of Jesus' teachings including His use of parables, as well as see the demonstration of His power over nature, evil spirits, sickness and even death itself.

Monday

Read Mark 4:1–20

Where did Jesus say that the sower's seed fell? What happened to the seed at each location? (Mark 4:3–8)

- path - fell & birds ate it
- Rocky = no depth of root
- thorns - choked it out - no grain
- other fell into good soil - grain produced ↑ 30, 60, 100 fold

What was the reason that Jesus gave the disciples and those around Him concerning why He used parables? (Mark 4:10–12)

To you (disciples) has been given the secret of the kingdom of God - for those outside all is parables.

In this parable, what type of people did each of the locations where the seed fell represent? (Mark 4:14–20)

The sower sows "the word" Jesus -
heart 1st / Satan comes - takes away
when hear it receive é joy = but NO root in themselves
endure for a while but will fall away
thorns are cares of world / deceitfulness of riches + desire for other things / choke the word -

good - hear word & accept it!

Tuesday

Read Mark 4:21–41

What was the analogy that Jesus used when telling His followers that whatever was hidden was meant to be made manifest? Why are we told to pay attention to what we hear? (Mark 4:21–25)

the light should shine for all.
nothing is hidden
no secrets
pay attention to what we hear = measured to you + more.
So if we hear Jesus' & allow his light to shine through me, & pay ↑ attention then more will be given to spread about.
multiplier effect

What do the parables of the scattered seed and the mustard seed have in common? (Mark 4:26–32)

- *Kingdom of God / scatter seed — God does the nature the rest*
- *Kingdom of God — through small seed grows to become > all other religions so we can rest in it*

What does the story of Jesus calming the storm tell us about Jesus and His disciples? (Mark 4:35–41)

faith / fear conflict
Jesus showed his fatigue human but divinity — power over nature
"Peace - Be still"
great calm

Wednesday

Read Mark 5

How did Jesus heal the man with an unclean spirit? (Mark 5:6–13)

words - come out of the man unclean spirit — Legion
gave "them" permission to enter pigs
≠ 2,000 pigs - drowned in sea

Go - tell your friends — Who was that?
tell how much [Lord] has done for you
how he has mercy on you —
He went to Decapolis

Jesus — Lord — same here

What does this passage tell us about the woman who touched Jesus' garment? (Mark 5:24–34)

faith made her well = Even if I touch him I will be healed
go in peace & be healed -
(power) had gone out from Jesus ...

How did Jesus respond to Jairus' plea for his dying daughter? (Mark 5:35–43)

no one should know → ruler of synagogue (Jairus)
father mother
Peter, James & John + Jairus — believed already.

Thursday
Read Mark 6:1–29

According to this passage who was astonished and why? What did Jesus say about His hometown and how was He hindered in ministry there? (Mark 6:1–6)

Who did the different people in this passage think that Jesus was? What did Herod say about it? (Mark 6:14–16)

Why did Herod's wife Herodias nurse a grudge against John the Baptist? Why was Herod hesitant to kill John the Baptist? (Mark 6:17–20)

Friday

Read Mark 6:30–56

How did Jesus respond to the crowd that followed Him? What analogy did He use to describe these people? (Mark 6:31–34)

How much food did the disciples have to feed the crowd? How many leftovers did they have after everyone ate? (Mark 6:38–44)

Why was Jesus delayed in getting to the boat to meet His disciples? What was their response when they saw Him walking on the water? How did Jesus respond to them? (Mark 6:45–51)

Saturday
Read Mark 7
What did Jesus say the Pharisees and scribes were guilty of doing? What example did Jesus use to back up His point? (Mark 7:9–13)

What did Jesus say defiles people? What examples did Jesus give? (Mark 7:14–23)

How did Jesus heal the deaf man with a speech impediment? How did people react to this healing? (Mark 7:32–37)

Week 3 — This week's Bible reading continues a walk through the Gospel of Mark. We'll look at Jesus feeding the four thousand, Jesus healing the blind, and Jesus foretelling His death and resurrection. We'll also look at the transfiguration and Jesus' teachings.

Monday

Read Mark 8:1–26

What was Jesus' motivation for performing this miracle? How much food did the disciples have before and after the people were fed? How many people ate? (Mark 8:1–10)

What did the disciples think that Jesus was talking about when He referred to the leaven of the Pharisees? What miracles did Jesus mention in response? (Mark 8:14–21)

How did Jesus heal the blind man at Bethsaida? (Mark 8:22–26)

Tuesday

Read Mark 8:27–38

Who did the people think that Jesus was? Who did Peter think that Jesus was? (Mark 8:27–29)

What did Jesus reveal to His disciples about His future? How did Peter respond to this information? How did Jesus respond to Peter? (Mark 8:31–33)

What did Jesus teach the crowd and His disciples about the cost of discipleship? (Mark 8:34–38)

Wednesday

Read Mark 9:1–32

What does this passage tell us about Jesus' transfiguration? What did the voice from the cloud say? What did Jesus tell Peter, James, and John to do concerning what they had witnessed? (Mark 9:2–10)

What did Jesus tell the father of the boy who was possessed by a mute spirit? How did Jesus drive the demon out? What happened to the boy? (Mark 9:23–27)

What did Jesus tell His disciples concerning the boy who was possessed by a mute spirit? (Mark 9:28–29)

23

Thursday

Read Mark 9:33–50

What did Jesus tell His disciples was the path to greatness? What brought about this conversation? (Mark 9:33–37)

service to little ones — unfortunate, marginalized poor.

What did Jesus tell His disciples about others who were doing ministry in His name? (Mark 9:38–41)

Leave them be

What was the message that Jesus gave His disciples concerning sin? What does this teaching reveal about the kingdom of God and about hell? (Mark 9:42–48)

we all are tempted but trials preserve us — we are sprinkled i salt / Jesus & holy spirit

Friday

Read Mark 10:1–31

What was the reason that Jesus gave the Pharisees concerning why Moses permitted a man to write a certificate of divorce? What does Jesus explain was God's intention for marriage from the beginning? (Mark 10:2–9)

hardness of heart

1:1 ♂ ♀

leave + cleave =

What was Jesus' response to the disciples for rebuking people bringing children to Him? How did Jesus respond to the children? (Mark 10:13–16)

What did the rich man want? What was Jesus' instructions to him? What analogy did Jesus use in describing this situation? (Mark 10:17–25)

Saturday
Read Mark 10:32–52

What details did Jesus give His disciples concerning what was about to happen to Him in Jerusalem? (Mark 10:32–34)

What did James and John request of Jesus? How did the other disciples respond to this request? What did Jesus teach His disciples as a result of this request? (Mark 10:35–45)

What was Bartimaeus' response to Jesus' presence? How did the crowd respond to Bartimaeus? How did Jesus respond to Bartimaeus? (Mark 10:46–52)

Week 4 — This week's Bible reading concludes our walk through the Gospel of Mark. This week we'll look at Jesus clearing the temple, the Parable of the Tenants, the signs of the end of the age, and Jesus' betrayal, trial, death, burial, and resurrection.

Monday

Read Mark 11

What did Jesus do upon entering the temple? What did Jesus proclaim concerning God's temple? How did the chief priests and scribes respond to this? (Mark 11:15–19)

What happened that Jesus cursed the fig tree? What did Jesus teach His disciples in response to this? (Mark 11:12–14, 20–25)

What was Jesus questioned about by the religious leaders? How did He respond? (Mark 11:27–33)

Tuesday

Read Mark 12:1–27

Who are the main players in this parable? What was Jesus trying to teach in this parable? (Mark 12:1–12)

Who came to Jesus questioning Him about paying taxes to Caesar? Why did they do this? How did Jesus respond to them? (Mark 12:13–17)

What did the Sadducees question Jesus about? What was the reason Jesus gave as to why they were in error? What did Jesus teach about marriage and the resurrection? (Mark 12:18–27)

Wednesday

Read Mark 12:28–44

What did Jesus say was the greatest commandment? What did He say was the second greatest commandment? What did the scribe, who asked the question, say about these commandments? (Mark 12:28–34)

What warning did Jesus give concerning the scribes? (Mark 12:38–40)

What did Jesus say about the poor widow who made an offering at the temple? What does this tell us about God's perspective on giving? (Mark 12:41–44)

Thursday

Read Mark 13

What did Jesus say were but the beginning of the birth pains? (Mark 13:6–8)

What are some of the characteristics of the end-time period? What must first happen with the Gospel? What does Jesus say about betrayal and hatred in these times? (Mark 13:9–13)

How does Jesus describe the final days and the suffering that will be on the earth at that time? How will Jesus return to earth and what will happen when He does return? (Mark 13:19–27)

Friday

Read Mark 14

Who anointed Jesus? What was used to anoint Him and what was the value of the item? How did Jesus respond to the complaint against the person? (Mark 14:3–9)

What did Peter boast? What was Jesus' response to this boast? How did Peter respond to Jesus? (Mark 14:27–31)

What did Jesus pray in Gethsemane? What did He tell Peter about prayer, the spirit, and the flesh? (Mark 14:32–38)

Saturday

Read Mark 15–16

How did the soldiers treat Jesus? How did the passersby, the religious leaders, and those crucified with Him treat Jesus when He was being crucified? (Mark 15:16–20, 29–32)

What happened when Jesus died on the cross? Who came to Pilate for Jesus' body? Who attested to Pilate of Jesus' death? Who witnessed Jesus' burial? (Mark 15:37–39, 43–47)

Who came to the tomb very early on the first day of the week? What did they witness when they arrived? What were they told about Jesus? (Mark 16:1–7)

Week 5 — This week's Bible reading begins our walk through the book of 1 Corinthians. We'll look at division in the church, what is taught about the cross and God's power, the wisdom of this age, the work of the Holy Spirit, pride, judgment and sexual sin.

Monday

Read 1 Corinthians 1

In what specific ways had the Corinthians been enriched? What did they not lack, and for what were they awaiting? What promise was given them? (1 Corinthians 1:4–9)

What problem was the church experiencing? What was God's counsel and desire for them? (1 Corinthians 1:10–11)

What do we learn about the word of the cross? How does Paul describe how Jews and Gentiles responded to his preaching Christ crucified? How are we who are called to see the preaching of Christ crucified? (1 Corinthians 1:18, 23–24)

Tuesday

Read 1 Corinthians 2

How did Paul preach the Gospel to the Corinthians? Where should our faith rest? (1 Corinthians 2:1–5)

Who did Paul preach wisdom to at Corinth? What was the nature of this wisdom? (1 Corinthians 2:6–9)

What does this passage teach us about the Holy Spirit? (1 Corinthians 2:10–13)

Wednesday
Read 1 Corinthians 3

How are people of the flesh defined? What were clear indications of this among the Corinthians? What analogy is used to refocus the church on who they should follow? (1 Corinthians 3:1–9)

What warning is given to "builders" in this passage? What is said must be the foundation of all spiritual building? How will all work be tested and when? (1 Corinthians 3:10–15)

What counsel is given to those who think they are wise by the standards of this age? What does God consider the wisdom of this world to be? (1 Corinthians 3:18–19)

Thursday

Read 1 Corinthians 4

What is mentioned here about judgment? (1 Corinthians 4:1–5)

What is being taught about pride in these verses? (1 Corinthians 4:6–7)

How is the life and ministry of an apostle described? (1 Corinthians 4:9–13)

Friday
Read 1 Corinthians 5

What problem was the church having? How did some in the church react to this issue? According to this passage how should have they reacted? (1 Corinthians 5:1–2)

How are the old leaven and unleavened bread defined in this passage? (1 Corinthians 5:6–8)

What instructions are given to the church about associating with immoral people? What groups are included? (1 Corinthians 5:9–11)

Saturday

Read 1 Corinthians 6

Who does this passage say are "saints" and what will they do in the future? (1 Corinthians 6:1–3)

What is taught about the unrighteous in this passage? Who is specifically included in this group? What happened to those who once lived like this but who had turned to Christ? (1 Corinthians 6:9–11)

What is taught in this passage about sexual immorality and the body? (1 Corinthians 6:12–20)

Week 6 — This week's Bible reading continues our walk through the book of 1 Corinthians. We will look at marriage, deference to the weaker conscience, material provision for ministers, temptation, and the Lord's Supper.

Monday

Read 1 Corinthians 7:1–16

What is mentioned about marital duty, authority of our bodies in marriage, and mutual consent for prayer? Who does Paul say instigates sexual temptation and what weakness of ours allows this? (1 Corinthians 7:1–5)

What wisdom is given concerning widows and the unmarried? (1 Corinthians 7:8–9)

What command does the Lord give here? What counsel does Paul give by the Holy Spirit to those who have unbelieving spouses? (1 Corinthians 7:10–16)

Tuesday

Read 1 Corinthians 7:17–40

What does Paul tell those who believe to do? What conditions of life does he address? (1 Corinthians 7:17–24)

What are we told about the married and unmarried? What is the goal, whether married or not? (1 Corinthians 7:32–35)

What is mentioned about the length of the marriage covenant and freedom to remarry? (1 Corinthians 7:39–40)

Wednesday
Read 1 Corinthians 8

What are we taught about knowledge and love? (1 Corinthians 8:1–3)

What are we told about God in this passage? (1 Corinthians 8:4–6)

What are we told we should take care about? What example is used to demonstrate how a person in that day with a weaker conscience could be destroyed by another's exercise of freedom? (1 Corinthians 8:9–13)

Thursday
Read 1 Corinthians 9
What analogies are used to build the case for material provision being given to a minister of the gospel? What has the Lord commanded concerning this? (1 Corinthians 9:7–14)

What does Paul explain was his reward in preaching the gospel? (1 Corinthians 9:15–18)

How did Paul approach winning people to Christ? How are we counseled to run our race? (1 Corinthians 9:19–27)

Friday
Read 1 Corinthians 10
What examples are used to warn us to not desire evil? (1 Corinthians 10:6–10)

What are we taught about temptation? (1 Corinthians 10:12–13)

How does Paul summarize in verse 31–33 what is being taught in verses 23–30? (1 Corinthians 10:31–33)

Saturday

Read 1 Corinthians 11

What were the underlying problems bringing about the issues mentioned in this passage? Why is this not the Lord's Supper? (1 Corinthians 11:17–22)

What specifics are relayed to us concerning the Lord's Supper? (1 Corinthians 11:23–26)

What are we warned about concerning the Lord's Supper? How are we instructed to partake of it? (1 Corinthians 11:27–34)

Thank you for making it this far! A quick review on Amazon would mean a lot! Just use your phone's camera on the QR code to leave a review →

Week 7 — This week's Bible reading concludes our walk through the book of 1 Corinthians. We'll look at spiritual gifts, the prime importance of love, the message of the gospel, and death and the resurrected body.

Monday
Read 1 Corinthians 12
What is God's will for us concerning spiritual gifts? Why is the manifestation of the Spirit given? What spiritual gifts are listed in this passage? (1 Corinthians 12:1–10)

What are the main things we should understand concerning the analogy of the human body and how it relates to how God has arranged the church? (1 Corinthians 12:14–20)

What are we told about having a part in Christ's body? What did God appoint in the church? What are we counseled to earnestly desire? (I Corinthians 12:27–31)

45

Tuesday

Read 1 Corinthians 13

What are we being taught here about gifts and love? What gifts and services are used as examples? (1 Corinthians 13:1–3)

What are the qualities of love stated in these verses? (1 Corinthians 13:4–7)

What are we told about the duration of spiritual gifts and knowledge? What does verse 12 say about our ability to see now? What are the three that abide and which is the greatest? (1 Corinthians 13:8–13)

Wednesday
Read 1 Corinthians 14

What are we told immediately concerning love and spiritual gifts? What is mentioned about prophecy? What is mentioned about tongues? (1 Corinthians 14:1–5)

What counsel is given about being eager for manifestations of the Spirit? What counsel is given to those who speak in tongues? (1 Corinthians 14:12–13)

What else do we learn about tongues and prophecy and Paul's instructions for their orderly operation in the church? (1 Corinthians 14:26–33)

Thursday

Read 1 Corinthians 15:1–49

What was the gospel that Paul preached? How many people did Jesus appear to after His resurrection? (1 Corinthians 15:1–8)

What does Paul say the problem is with not believing in the resurrection? When will those who believe be resurrected? What will Christ destroy when He returns? (1 Corinthians 15:16–26)

List the description of our current bodies and the contrasting description of our resurrected bodies? Ultimately whose likeness shall we bear? (1 Corinthians 15:42–49)

Friday

Read 1 Corinthians 15:50–58

How exactly will the dead be raised? When will this occur? (1 Corinthians 15:50–53)

What can we learn about death from this passage? As Christians, why can we be joyful in the face of death? (1 Corinthians 15:54–57)

In light of our eternal state, how are we told to live? Why should we always abound in the work of the Lord? (1 Corinthians 15:58)

Saturday
Read 1 Corinthians 16

What instructions were given to the Corinthians concern the offering being taken? What was the purpose of the offering? What does this passage teach us about the church's and individual believer's role in giving? (1 Corinthians 16:1–4)

What specific instructions were given in these verses? (1 Corinthians 16:13–14)

Who were the first converts in Achaia? To what were they devoted? What did Paul urge the church to do toward these and toward those who labored in this work? (1 Corinthians 16:15–16)

Week 8 — This week's Bible reading begins our walk through the book of 2 Corinthians. We will look at the comfort that God gives, forgiveness, the ministry of the Spirit, Paul's ministry, and the effects of reconciliation in the life of believers.

Monday

Read 2 Corinthians 1

List out what we learn about comfort from this passage. (2 Corinthians 1:3–7)

What are we told about the affliction Paul suffered? Why does it say this happened? What are we told about prayer? (2 Corinthians 1:8–11)

Do your best to rewrite/paraphrase these verses in your own words. (2 Corinthians 1:21–22)

Tuesday
Read 2 Corinthians 2

Why did Paul not go back to Corinth? What reason did Paul give for writing his initial letter? What did Paul say about his emotional state when he wrote them? (2 Corinthians 2:1–4)

What were the instructions to the Corinthians concerning forgiving the one who had fallen into sin? Why was it important for the church to apply mercy to the one who had fallen? (2 Corinthians 2:5–8)

What are we told about Paul's ministry and the fragrance they were to those who were being saved and to those who were perishing? How did Paul minister the word of God? (2 Corinthians 2:14–17)

Wednesday
Read 2 Corinthians 3

Summarize what are we told about the ministry of the Spirit in these verses. (2 Corinthians 3:7–11)

What is said about the veil that lies over the heart? How is this veil taken away? (2 Corinthians 3:14–16)

What are we told about the Spirit? How are believers being transformed? (2 Corinthians 3:17–18)

Thursday
Read 2 Corinthians 4

What are some of the characteristics of Paul's ministry? Who does Paul say that the gospel is veiled? What is the reason as to why this happens? (2 Corinthians 4:1–4)

What are we told that Paul believed that motivated him to speak? (2 Corinthians 4:13–14)

Describe why Paul did not lose heart. What was his focus? (2 Corinthians 4:16–18)

Friday
Read 2 Corinthians 5
Contrast the terms Paul uses to describe a believer's earthly and heavenly bodies. What do we have as a guarantee of what is to come? (2 Corinthians 5:1–5)

How are we called to walk? Where did Paul prefer to be? What is our aim as believers? (2 Corinthians 5:7–9)

List the encouragements contained in this passage concerning those who are in Christ. Who are we now in Christ? (2 Corinthians 5:17–21)

Saturday
Read 2 Corinthians 6

What does this passage teach us concerning the favorable time and salvation? (2 Corinthians 6:1–2)

List out how Paul commended himself to the Corinthians and the difficulties he endured. (2 Corinthians 6:4–10)

Summarize what this passage teaches concerning the yoking of believers with unbelievers. (2 Corinthians 6:14–18)

Week 9 — This week's Bible reading concludes our walk through the book of 2 Corinthians. We will look at Paul's love and concern for the believers, generosity in giving, his defense of his ministry, and his thorn in the flesh.

Monday

Read 2 Corinthians 7

What did Paul request of the believers? What was his attitude toward the believers at Corinth? (2 Corinthians 7:2–4)

How did Paul describe their condition when they came into Macedonia? Who did Paul say that God comforts? How did God comfort them in this situation? (2 Corinthians 7:5–7)

Contrast the difference between godly grief and worldly grief. What characteristics of godly grief are listed in this passage? (2 Corinthians 7:10–11)

Tuesday

Read 2 Corinthians 8

List out what this passage tells us about the Macedonian churches. (2 Corinthians 8:1–5)

What does Paul's teach about giving in these verses? (2 Corinthians 8:12–14)

What did Paul do to ensure the generous gift was administered properly? In whose sight was he desiring to do what is honorable? (2 Corinthians 8:17–21)

Wednesday
Read 2 Corinthians 9
What were the Corinthians ready to do? Why did Paul send the "brothers"? What was the end goal of Paul's advance notice? (2 Corinthians 9:1–5)

What truths did Paul share with the Corinthians concerning giving in this passage? (2 Corinthians 9:6–8)

List out the benefits Paul shared that would result from the generosity of God's people. (2 Corinthians 9:12–14)

Thursday
Read 2 Corinthians 10

What kind of weapons are we told that we possess and what power do they have? What are these weapons used for? (2 Corinthians 10:3–6)

What did some say concerning Paul? How did Paul respond to this accusation? (2 Corinthians 10:10–11)

Who did Paul say was without understanding? What was Paul's hope? What did Paul have to say about boasting? (2 Corinthians 10:12–18)

Friday

Read 2 Corinthians 11

What was Paul afraid of concerning the church at Corinth? What was the basis for this concern? (2 Corinthians 11:1–4)

What does this passage teach us about Satan and his servants? (2 Corinthians 11:13–15)

List out what this passage tells us concerning the sufferings that Paul faced for the gospel. (2 Corinthians 11:23–28)

Saturday

Read 2 Corinthians 12–13

What facts are we told concerning the thorn in Paul's flesh? What was Paul's response to God's word to him? With what did Paul become content and why? (2 Corinthians 12:7–10)

What did Paul fear he would find among the believers when he arrived at Corinth? (2 Corinthians 12:20–21)

According to this passage, why did Paul write this letter? What was the purpose for the authority that the Lord gave to him? (2 Corinthians 13:10)

Week 10 — This week's Bible reading will begin our walk through the book of 2 Samuel. We'll look at David and Saul's death, David as king of Judah, the war, Abner's murder, Ish-Bosheth's murder, David as king of Israel, and the ark of God brought to the City of David.

Monday

Read 2 Samuel 1

How did David learn of Saul's death? Who said that he killed Saul when Saul was discovered leaning on his spear? What did this person bring to David that Saul had? (2 Samuel 1:1–10)

How did David and his men react to the news of Saul's death? Who are we told they mourned for and how did they mourn? What did David do to the one who brought the news of Saul's death? (2 Samuel 1:11–16)

Look at the song of lament that David wrote for Saul and Jonathan. What stands out to you about this lament? (2 Samuel 1:17–27)

Tuesday

Read 2 Samuel 2

What did David do after Saul had died that brought him to Hebron? Who went with him to settle in Hebron and what happened to David there? (2 Samuel 2:1–4)

Who was the leader of Saul's army and what did he do after Saul's death? Over whom did this new ruler reign and for how long? How long are we told that David reigned over only the house of Judah? (2 Samuel 2:8–11)

How did the battle between the house of David and the house of Saul begin? Who was killed in the initial battle that was a prominent person and how did this happen? (2 Samuel 2:12–23)

Wednesday
Read 2 Samuel 3

Why was Abner moved to hand the kingdom of Saul and all Israel over to David? (2 Samuel 3:6–12)

What did David demand of Abner before he could come into his presence? What did Abner do to prepare the way to hand Israel over to David? (2 Samuel 3:13–21)

How was Abner murdered, why and by whom? How did David initially react to Abner's murder? (2 Samuel 3:22–29)

Thursday
Read 2 Samuel 4

What was the reaction of Ish-Bosheth and all Israel over Abner's death? Who were Rechab and Baanah? What do we learn about Mephibosheth? (2 Samuel 4:1–4)

Summarize what Rechab and Baanah did. (2 Samuel 4:5–8)

How did David react to Rechab and Baanah's actions? (2 Samuel 4:9–12)

Friday

Read 2 Samuel 5

Who came to make David king of Israel? What reasoning did they give David for making him king? How old was David when he became king of Judah? How old was he when he became king of Israel? (2 Samuel 5:1–5)

What city did David capture? What was the attitude of those who dwelt there toward David capturing their city? Who helped David by building a house for him? (2 Samuel 5:6–11)

What did the Philistines do when they learned that David had been anointed king? How did David react and what was the outcome? How did David react to the Philistines' second incursion? (2 Samuel 5:17–25)

Saturday
Read 2 Samuel 6

Who did David gather to bring up the ark of God to the City of David? How did they transport the ark? What were the people and David doing? (2 Samuel 6:1–5)

What happened as they were transporting the ark? Who died and what are we told was the reason? How did David react to this event and where did the ark stay? What happened to this person's house? (2 Samuel 6:6–11)

What was David told that motivated him to bring the ark of God to the City of David? Summarize how David acted during this occasion and contrast how Michal acted. (2 Samuel 6:12–23)

Week 11 — This week's Bible reading will continue our walk through the book of 2 Samuel. We'll look at God's promise to David, David's victories, David and Mephibosheth, the defeat of the Ammonites, David and Bathsheba, and Nathan's confrontation of David.

Monday

Read 2 Samuel 7

What did David want to do for the ark of God? How did Nathan the prophet initially respond to David's desire in this matter? What did the LORD say to Nathan the prophet that night about what David wanted to do? (2 Samuel 7:1–7)

What did the LORD say he had done and would do for David, the people, and David's heir? (Hint: look for the word "I") (2 Samuel 7:8–16)

What does David say in his prayer about the people of Israel? (2 Samuel 7:23–24)

Tuesday

Read 2 Samuel 8

Who did David defeat and subdue in the course of time? What other people are we told that David defeated? How did he treat them? (2 Samuel 8:1–2)

What other great victory are we told about? What plunder did David take to Jerusalem and who did he devote all the dedicated things to? (2 Samuel 8:3–12)

What battle made David famous and where did it take place? What resulted from this battle and what are we told about the Lord's hand in all these victories? What are we told about David's reign? (2 Samuel 8:13–15)

Wednesday
Read 2 Samuel 9

What was David's question and why did he ask it? Who came to David and what did David find out? (2 Samuel 9:1–4)

What did David do for Mephibosheth? (2 Samuel 9:5–7)

What else did David do for Jonathan's son Mephibosheth? (2 Samuel 9:9–10)

Thursday

Read 2 Samuel 10

What happened that caused David to send a delegation to the Ammonites? How were David's men treated? (2 Samuel 10:1–5)

What did the Ammonites do after this incident? How did David respond? What happened in this initial battle? (2 Samuel 10:6–14)

How did the second battle unfold? What part did David play in this battle and what was the outcome? (2 Samuel 10:15–19)

Friday
Read 2 Samuel 11

Where was David during the springtime when kings were to go off to battle? Who did David see bathing, what did he do, and what was the result? (2 Samuel 11:1–5)

What did David try to do to hide the evidence of his sin? (2 Samuel 11:6–13)

What did David do next when his first plan to hide his sin failed? What are we told about the Lord's thoughts of David's actions? (2 Samuel 11:14–17, 26–27)

Saturday

Read 2 Samuel 12

What story did Nathan use to bring David's sin to light? How did David initially react to the story? (2 Samuel 12:1–6)

What did Nathan prophesy to David after telling him the story? (2 Samuel 12:7–14)

What immediately happened within David's family? How did David react to this event? Why did David fast? (2 Samuel 12:15–18, 22–23)

Week 12 — This week's Bible reading will continue our walk through the book of 2 Samuel. We will look at Amnon and Tamar, Absalom's return to Jerusalem, Absalom's conspiracy, David's flight from Jerusalem, and Absalom's death.

Monday

Read 2 Samuel 13

How did Amnon deceive King David so that he could get Tamar alone? Whose advice did he take? (2 Samuel 13:1–6)

How long did Absalom wait to take revenge on Amnon? How did Absalom plot Amnon's murder? (2 Samuel 13:23–29)

How did David initially respond to the news of the possible slaughter? Who was it that set David straight on what had happened? Where did Absalom go and for how long? How did King David feel about this? (2 Samuel 13:30–39)

Tuesday

Read 2 Samuel 14

Who devised the plan to bring Absalom back to Jerusalem? Why did he do this? Who did he employ to execute the plan? (2 Samuel 14:1–3)

What are we told about Absalom? How long did he live in Jerusalem before seeing King David's face? (2 Samuel 14:23–28)

What did Absalom do to get Joab's attention so that he would see the king? What was the outcome of his actions? (2 Samuel 14:29–33)

Wednesday

Read 2 Samuel 15

Summarize how Absalom stole the hearts of the men of Israel. (2 Samuel 15:1–6)

What did David do when he found out about the conspiracy? (2 Samuel 15:13–18)

How did David and his people leave Jerusalem? What was David's strategy to foil the advice of Ahithophel? (2 Samuel 15:30–34)

Thursday

Read 2 Samuel 16

Who met David with donkeys and supplies? What did he tell David about Mephibosheth? How did David reward Ziba? (2 Samuel 16:1–4)

Who was Shimei and what did he do to David and his officials? How did David respond to Abishai's desire to kill Shimei? In what state did David and the people arrive at their destination? (2 Samuel 16:5–14)

What advice did Ahithophel give Absalom upon his entrance into Jerusalem and why? What are we told about Ahithophel? (2 Samuel 16:20–23)

Friday

Read 2 Samuel 17

What advice did Ahithophel give to Absalom and what was the immediate response to the advice? Why did Absalom not immediately act on Ahithophel's advice? (2 Samuel 17:1–6)

What advice did Hushai, King David's friend, give to Absalom? How did Absalom and the men of Israel react to Hushai's advice? Why are we told that they reacted this way? (2 Samuel 17:7–14)

What did Ahithophel do when he realized that his advice was no longer being taken? (2 Samuel 17:23)

Saturday

Read 2 Samuel 18

Who did David put in command of his men and what did he tell his commanders concerning Absalom? (2 Samuel 18:1–5)

Where did the battle take place, what was the outcome, and how exactly did Absalom die? (2 Samuel 18:6–15)

What was King David's reaction to Absalom's death? (2 Samuel 18:31–33)

Week 13 — This week's Bible reading will conclude our walk through the book of 2 Samuel. We'll look at David's return to Jerusalem, the rebellion of Sheba son of Bicri, David's song of praise, David's mighty men, and David's sin of counting the fighting men.

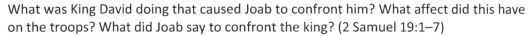
Monday

Read 2 Samuel 19

What was King David doing that caused Joab to confront him? What affect did this have on the troops? What did Joab say to confront the king? (2 Samuel 19:1–7)

Who came to help King David cross the Jordan? What did Shimei do when he came to David? How did Abishai respond concerning Shimei? What did David say to Shimei? (2 Samuel 19:15–23)

Who was Barzillai and what did he do for David? What did David want to do in response to Barzillai's kindness? How did Barzillai respond to this offer? (2 Samuel 19:31–37)

Tuesday

Read 2 Samuel 20

Who rose up against David and drew Israel away from David? Who killed Amasa and how did this happen? (2 Samuel 20:1–2, 6–10)

Where did Sheba son of Bicri go? Who pursued him and what did they do to the city? Who called out to speak with Joab from the city? (2 Samuel 20:14–16)

Summarize what the wise woman said and did that saved her town from Joab and David's army? (2 Samuel 20:17–22)

Wednesday

Read 2 Samuel 21

Why was there a three-year famine in the land? How did David find out the cause of the famine? What did David do in response once he had heard from the LORD? (2 Samuel 21:1–6)

What did the Gibeonites do to the seven descendants of King Saul? Who was Rizpah and what did she do? How did King David react to Rizpah's actions? (2 Samuel 21:8–14)

What happened in the battle between the Philistines and Israel? (2 Samuel 21:15–17)

Thursday

Read 2 Samuel 22

Define in your own words each term David uses to describe the LORD. (2 Samuel 22:2–3)

What did God do for David? (2 Samuel 22:17–20)

What are some other things that David praised God for? (2 Samuel 22:33–37)

Friday

Read 2 Samuel 23
What did God reveal to David in these verses? (2 Samuel 23:2–4)

What did Eleazar do in battle? (2 Samuel 23:9–10)

Who was Benaiah and what did he do in battle? (2 Samuel 23:20–23)

Saturday

Read 2 Samuel 24

Why did David count the fighting men? How did Joab react to this command from King David? (2 Samuel 24:1–4)

How many fighting men were there in Israel and Judah at that time? What happened to David when he heard the report? Who came to David the next morning to confront him about this? (2 Samuel 24:9–12)

What options did God give David as a result of his action of counting the fighting men? What did David choose and how many people died? What caused the LORD to relent? (2 Samuel 24:13–16)

Congrats on Finishing the workbook! Thank you!
Just use your phone's camera on the QR code to view our other workbooks!

Weekly Memory Verses

Week 1 — Mark 3:35 — "For whoever does the will of God, he is my brother and sister and mother." (ESV)

Week 2 — Mark 5:19 — "And he did not permit him but said to him, 'Go home to your friends and tell them how much the Lord has done for you, and how he has had mercy on you.'" (ESV)

Week 3 — Mark 10:27 — "Jesus looked at them and said, 'With man it is impossible, but not with God. For all things are possible with God.'" (ESV)

Week 4 — Mark 12:30–31 – "'And you shall love the Lord your God with all your heart and with all your soul and with all your mind and with all your strength.' The second is this: 'You shall love your neighbor as yourself.' There is no other commandment greater than these." (ESV)

Week 5 — 1 Corinthians 1:8 — "who will sustain you to the end, guiltless in the day of our Lord Jesus Christ." (ESV)

Week 6 — 1 Corinthians 8:6 — "…yet for us there is one God, the Father, from whom are all things and for whom we exist, and one Lord, Jesus Christ, through whom are all things and through whom we exist." (ESV)

Week 7 — 1 Corinthians 15:20 — "But in fact Christ has been raised from the dead, the first-fruits of those who have fallen asleep." (ESV)

Week 8 — 2 Corinthians 5:17 — "Therefore, if anyone is in Christ, he is a new creation. The old has passed away; behold, the new has come." (ESV)

Week 9 — 2 Corinthians 12:9 — "But he said to me, 'My grace is sufficient for you, for my power is made perfect in weakness.' Therefore I will boast all the more gladly of my weaknesses, so that the power of Christ may rest upon me." (ESV)

Week 10 — 2 Samuel 6:5 — "And David and all the house of Israel were celebrating before the Lord, with songs and lyres and harps and tambourines and castanets and cymbals." (ESV)

Week 11 — 2 Samuel 7:22 — "Therefore you are great, O Lord God. For there is none like you, and there is no God besides you, according to all that we have heard with our ears." (ESV)

Week 12 — 2 Samuel 14:14 — "We must all die; we are like water spilled on the ground, which cannot be gathered up again. But God will not take away life, and he devises means so that the banished one will not remain an outcast." (ESV)

Week 13— 2 Samuel 22:31 — "This God—his way is perfect; the word of the Lord proves true; he is a shield for all those who take refuge in him." (ESV)

Journal & Notes

Journal & Notes

Journal & Notes

Journal & Notes

Journal & Notes

Journal & Notes

Journal & Notes

Journal & Notes

Journal & Notes

Journal & Notes

Journal & Notes

Journal & Notes

Journal & Notes

Made in United States
North Haven, CT
18 June 2024

53788968R00057